KIDS THROUGHOUT HISTORY™

Kids in Ancient Greece

Lisa A. Wroble

· The Rosen Publishing Group's
PowerKids Press™
New York

Published in 1997 by The Rosen Publishing Group, Inc.
29 East 21st Street, New York, NY 10010

First Edition

Book design: Danielle Primiceri

Photo credits: Cover © Corbis-Bettmann (left), © Archive Photos (right); p. 4 © Archivi Alinari 1991/Art Resource; pp. 7, 8, 16, 20 © Archive Photos; p. 11 © Gian Berto Vanni/Art Resource; pp. 12, 15, 19 © Erich Lessing/Art Resource.

Wroble, Lisa A.
    Kids in ancient Greece / Lisa A. Wroble.
        p.   cm. — (Kids throughout history)
    Includes index.
    Summary: Describes daily life in ancient Greece, discussing the home, clothing, food, families, education, and religion.
    ISBN 0-8239-5122-7
    1. Children—Greece—Juvenile literature. 2. Family—Greece—Juvenile literature. 3. Greece—Social life and customs—Juvenile literature. [1. Greece—Civilization.] I. Title. II. Series: Wroble, Lisa A. Kids throughout history.
    DF93.W76 1997
    938—dc21   96-52433
                                                                                                        CIP
                                                                                                        AC r97

Manufactured in the United States of America

Contents

Greek Civilization

Ancient (AYN-shent) Greece was a civilization (SIV-ul-ih-ZAY-shun) that lasted from 3000 B.C. to 146 B.C. **Modern** (MAH-dern) Greece is a country in Europe. But ancient Greece included all of Greece, parts of Italy, and areas around the Aegean Sea. The period of ancient Greece that we're going to look at was between 1200 B.C and 146 B.C.

Greek city-states were like little countries that shared the same language, religious beliefs, and customs. But they were not **united** (yoo-NY-ted) as one country.

Religion was a large part of the lives of the ancient Greeks. There are many statues of Greek gods. This statue shows the god Hercules as a child. He is strangling a serpent that was sent to kill him.

Cities

Ancient Greek city-states were large and often built on hills. Houses were built close together. Dirt or stone streets zigzagged up the hills to make it easier to climb to the **temples** (TEM-pulz), which were built at the top. An open space near the center of each city was called the *agora* (uh-GOR-uh). The *agora* was the market and the public meeting place. Each city also had a **gymnasium** (jim-NAY-zee-um), or an area for exercise and wrestling. Physical strength was important to the ancient Greeks.

A wall was built around many cities to keep people safe from thieves or during wars. This is a picture of ▶ the Greek city Olympia.

City-States

Castor was a Greek boy. He lived in the city-state of Athens. Each city-state was ruled by a **council** (KOWN-sil) of elders. People were **loyal** (LOY-ul) to their city-states rather than to what we now call the country of Greece. Most Greek city-states were run the same way. The councils all believed that education and religion were very important. One city-state, Sparta, was different from the rest. Strength was more important than education in Sparta. Boys and girls were trained from a young age to be strong and athletic.

This picture shows a flower market in the ancient city-state of Athens. Today, Athens is the capital of Greece.

Houses

Castor's house was made of bricks built on a stone floor. Clay tiles covered the roof. At the center of the house was a **courtyard** (KORT-yard). All the rooms of the house were built around the courtyard. Many houses had an altar to the gods in the courtyard. Light for the whole house came from a skylight, or an opening in the roof, which was over the courtyard.

Many houses and temples were built so well that they lasted for hundreds of years. You can see parts of some of these houses in Greece today. ▶

Clothing

Greek people wore **chitons** (KY-tunz). A *chiton* was made of two pieces of finely woven wool or linen cloth. The pieces were sewn together at the shoulders and along the tops of the arms. A belt around the waist held the *chiton* in place. Women's *chitons* were floor length. Boys, girls, and men wore knee-length *chitons*. A cloak called a **himation** (heh-MAT-ee-ahn) was draped or wrapped around the *chiton* and pinned at the shoulder. Most people wore leather sandals.

◄ *The men and women of ancient Greece wore the same type of clothing. But women's* chitons *were longer than men's.*

Food

Castor's father often held dinner parties. He ate with friends in the dining room. Castor was sometimes allowed to attend and listen to the men discuss different things. Women were not allowed to eat in the dining room. They ate in the kitchen with the children.

Men ate propped up on pillows on long couches. Food, such as grapes, olives, figs, eggs, fish, and bread, was placed on a low table. People ate with their fingers, taking food from serving bowls. They drank wine mixed with water.

The dining room in which the men ate was called the andron. ▶

Toys and Games

Children in ancient Greece played many games that were like the games children play today. Castor wrestled with his friends. He and other boys played with tops, toy sailboats, pull carts, and toy **chariots** (CHAYR-ee-ots). They pretended to have sword fights. Girls played with dolls and little houses made with clay furniture. They also played a game like jacks, using knuckle bones from animals. At the age of thirteen, children offered their toys to the gods at the temple. This was a sign of becoming an adult.

People often put on puppet shows, like the one shown here.

Education

Castor started school when he was seven years old. He learned to read, write, and do math. Castor scratched his lessons on a wax tablet. The wax could be scraped smooth and used again. Castor also had physical training in gym class. He learned to run fast, jump far, and wrestle. This helped him become strong.

Girls learned to read, write, and do math at home. To keep fit, girls ran, jumped, and wrestled with each other. Their mothers taught them to spin thread, and weave and sew cloth.

Many young people learned to play stringed instruments and flutes. ▶

Religion

The Greeks believed that gods and goddesses controlled everything in life, including the wind, water, and crops. Making a god or goddess angry could mean bad luck or even death. People gave offerings of wine, food, coins, or jewelry to ask a favor of or to give thanks to a god or goddess. Each city-state had a god or goddess of its own. These were chosen by the city council. A festival was held each year in honor of the city's god or goddess.

A person could ask a favor or give thanks to a god or goddess and leave an offering.

Social Life

Many customs from ancient Greece are still around today. To honor the gods and goddesses, the ancient Greeks held athletic **competitions** (kom-peh-TISH-unz) every year for adults and children. That was how the Olympic Games began. The ancient Greeks held speeches and acted out religious stories and beliefs. We still act out many Greek plays today. And then, as today, a healthy body was just as important as a good education. We owe many of the things we do to the people of ancient Greece.

Glossary

agora (uh-GOR-uh) An open market or meeting place.

ancient (AYN-shent) From a time long ago.

chariot (CHAYR-ee-ot) A two-wheeled carriage pulled by horses.

chiton (KY-tun) Two pieces of cloth sewn at the shoulder and worn with a belt around the waist.

civilization (SIV-ul-ih-ZAY-shun) The ways of living of a people or a country.

competition (kom-peh-TISH-un) A contest.

council (KOWN-sil) A group of people chosen by the people of a city-state to make laws for and be in charge of that city-state.

courtyard (KORT-yard) A space enclosed by walls in or near a building.

gymnasium (jim-NAY-zee-um) A room or building for physical exercises or training.

himation (heh-MAT-ee-ahn) A cloak that is wrapped around the body and pinned at the shoulder.

loyal (LOY-ul) True and faithful to someone or something.

modern (MAH-dern) Of the present day.

temple (TEM-pul) A place of worship.

united (yoo-NY-ted) Working together.

Index